66 I've learned the power of the word of a president. Not maybe necessarily to make—get something done, but the power of the word. **99**

12/22/91

BUSH-ISMS

COMPILED BY THE EDITORS OF
THE NEW REPUBLIC

Workman Publishing

The Bushisms were compiled by
Jonathan Bines and edited
by Andrew Sullivan and Jacob Weisberg

Copyright © 1992 The New Republic

Library of Congress Cataloging-in-Publication Data

Bushisms / compiled by the editors of the New republic.
p. cm.
ISBN 1-56305-318-7
1. Bush, George, 1924- —Quotations. 2. Bush, George, 1924-
—Humor. 3. United States—Politics and government—1989-
—Quotations, maxims, etc. 4. United States—Politics and
government—1989- —Humor. I. New republic (New York, N.Y.)
E838.5.B872   1992   92-15840
973.928′092—dc20   CIP

Workman books are available at special discounts when
purchased in bulk for premiums and sales promotions as
well as for fund-raising or educational use. Special
editions can also be created to specification. For details,
contact the Special Sales Director at the address below.

Workman Publishing Company, Inc.
708 Broadway
New York, NY 10003

Manufactured in the United States of America

First printing May 1992

10 9 8 7 6 5 4 3 2

An Introduction by Michael Kinsley

B y the end of Ronald Reagan's first term, supporters and opponents alike had begun to use the term "Reaganism" to refer to his governing ideology. But no one uses the term "Bushism" to mean any coherent set of political beliefs, or even a recognizable presidential style.

Instead, a "Bushism" has come to mean the incumbent's funny way of talking. The staccato sentences with no pronouns. The long, meandering non-sentences that reverse course or get lost completely halfway through. The fractured syntax. The weird mixed metaphors and non sequiturs.

But no one has yet explained convincingly why he talks this way or what it means. The editors at *The New Republic* have put together here a collection of 100 classic Bushisms. Reading these classics all at once does not solve the mystery, but it does shed some light.

Bush's rambly, semi-coherent style has been compared to Eisenhower's. Yet Eisenhower's verbiage lacked Bush's essential frantic quality. His admirers believed Ike could turn the fog machine on or off at will, and used it purposely to divert and confuse. No one has ever tried to make that case about Bush, so far.

The positive spin on Bushism is different. It's that his inarticulateness illustrates his sincerity and lack of artifice. It shows he's a regular guy, a small "d" democrat. Some of his silliest and most patently insincere babbling comes when he is trying to be demotic. ("When I need a little free advice about Saddam Hussein, I turn to country music.") The best case for Bushspeak as an expression of the democratic impulse was made by Jacob Weisberg of *The New Republic* who compared Bush to "a big, clumsy, golden retriever, drooling and knocking over furniture in his eagerness" to please everyone.

Timothy Noah of *The Wall Street Journal* compares Bush's strange discursiveness to call-waiting: Bush is always putting one half-finished thought on hold to take up the next one. Closely related to this is the intensely self-conscious tendency described by Meg Greenfield in *Newsweek:* "Bush is constantly telling you how to look at what he is doing, or what the impression is he is trying to create." ("We have—I have—want to be positioned in that I could not possibly support David Duke because of his racism and because of the bigotry and all of this.") What these tics share is a clear view of the mind at work. Bush's mental processes lie close to the surface.

This is honesty of a sort. Bush is famous for his attitude that politics is a distasteful business one stoops to when one has to. When he denies a remark he has just made ("People understand that Congress bears a greater responsibility for this—but I'm not trying to assign blame") or reads his stage directions aloud ("Message: I care"), he is telegraphing that he doesn't really mean what he says, that it's all just politics. It's sort of a verbal wink. The implication is that as long as we're all in on the joke, it doesn't matter.

But maybe it does matter. What Bush seems to have

no interest in is not just politics in the narrowest sense but political ideas of any kind. He is constantly revealing this in unconsciously dismissive references to "freedom and democracy and things of that nature". When he says, "I think in politics there are certain moral values. I'm one who—we believe strongly in pluralism...but when you get into some questions there are some moral overtones. Murder, that kind of thing...", he is pretty transparently faking it. The transparency is to his credit, in a way, but the faking it is not.

Bush's problem is not a lack of intelligence—or (as some have suggested) an excess of the tranquilizer Halcion. At bottom, his problem is a simple lack of anything to say. That's why he babbles. That's why he contradicts himself. That's why he tells you how you should perceive what he's saying, instead of just saying it. That's why he tells transparent whoppers.

A man anchored in true beliefs not only would be more articulate in expressing those beliefs, he would make a better liar, too. He wouldn't wreck a story about how faith sustained him while he waited to be rescued from the Pacific during World War II by adding, preposterously, that he was also sustained by thoughts of "the separation of church and state". Ronald Reagan, a man of a few, clear, rock-hard beliefs, was a brilliant liar.

If there were a real Bushism, in other words, there might not be all these Bushisms. Is that clear at all?

THE R-WORD

'I am less interested in what the definition is. You might argue technically, are we in a recession or not. But when there's this kind of sluggishness and concern— definitions, heck with it. **99**

— in an interview with WPVI-TV in Philadelphia.
12/17/91

66 **I** had a good long talk bilaterally with François Mitterrand this morning. 99

— during a news conference after the NATO summit in Rome, on the stability of the alliance in light of the divergent needs of its constituent members. 11/8/91

"If you're worried about caribou, take a look at the arguments that were used about the pipeline. They'd say the caribou would be extinct. You've got to shake them away with a stick. They're all making love lying up against the pipeline and you got thousands of caribou up there."

—at a Bush/Quayle '92 fundraiser in Houston, Texas, defending his plan to offer oil companies "environmentally responsive access" to the Alaskan National Wildlife Reserve. 10/31/91

66 If you want to have a philosophical
discussion, I take your point,
because I think it is important
that if we—if you presented me
with a hypothesis, 'You've got to do
this or you've got to do that,' and I
would accept it and understand the
political risks that'd be involved if I
showed any flexibility at all in even
discussing it—I would have to say
that—that a—that you make a very
valid point in your question, because,
as I tried to indicate in my remarks,
it's job creation, and that is attraction
of capital that is really the best
antidote to poverty. 99

—at the American Business
Conference in Washington,
D.C., on the unadvisability of
shifting the tax burden from
producers to consumers.
4/4/89

'I'm not the most articulate emotionalist. '

— at a question-and-answer session following the Malta summit with Gorbachev, when asked "what was it like for you sitting across from this man?" 12/3/89

> **"P**lease don't ask me to do that which I've just said I'm not going to do, because you're burning up time; the meter is running through the sand on you, and I am now filibustering. **"**

— during a press conference in the Oval Office, refusing to answer a reporter's persistent questions about the Oliver North trial.
4/20/89

"You cannot be president of the United States if you don't have faith. Remember Lincoln, going to his knees in times of trial and the Civil War and all that stuff. You can't be. And we are blessed. So don't feel sorry for—don't cry for me, Argentina."

— to employees of the Liberty
Mutual Insurance Company in
Dover, New Hampshire, while
campaigning before the New
Hampshire Primary, stressing
the importance of prayer.
1/15/92

7

66 The Democrats want to ram it down my ear in a political victory. 99

—at a Bush/Quayle '92 fund-raiser in Houston, Texas, accusing the Democrats of partisanship in negotiations over competing plans to extend unemployment benefits. 10/31/91

> **I** don't want to just sit here blaming Congress. I mean, we're all in this together.

— to news anchor Bill Stuart of
KCNC-TV, Denver
11/20/91

> I think the Congress should be blamed.

— Several minutes later, to Warner
Saunders of WMAQ-TV, Chicago

66 **I**'ve told you I don't live and die by the polls. Thus I will refrain from pointing out that we're not doing too bad in those polls. **99**

— during departure remarks before traveling to Rome for a NATO summit, on polls showing a decrease in the percentage of the electorate willing to vote to reelect him in 1992.
11/6/91

REPORTER: Do you know to what extent the U.S. and Colombia are in fact cooperating militarily now, in terms of interdiction efforts?

BUSH: Well I—Yes, I know that.

REPORTER: Can you share that with us?

BUSH: No.

REPORTER: Why not, sir?

BUSH: Because I don't feel like it.

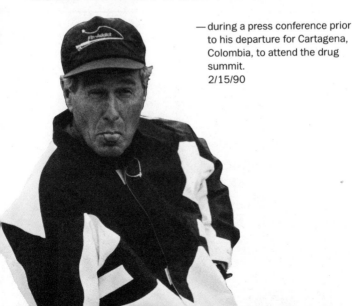

—during a press conference prior to his departure for Cartagena, Colombia, to attend the drug summit.
2/15/90

66 It has been said by some cynic, maybe it was a former president, 'If you want a friend in Washington, get a dog.' We took them literally—that advice—as you know. But I didn't need that, because I have Barbara Bush. 99

—to the American Association of Community and Junior Colleges Convention in Washington, D.C. The Convention had recognized the First Lady for her work promoting literacy. 3/30/89

'I'm delighted that Barbara Bush is with me today, and I—She got a good, clean bill of health yesterday from Walter Reed Hospital, I might add, and then—But I'm taking another look at our doctor. He told her it's okay to kiss the dog— I mean—no—it's okay to kiss your husband, but don't kiss the dog. So I don't know exactly what that means.'

— during a speech, "Project Education Reform: Time for Results," delivered at a Union, New Jersey, high school. Bush, who once said his wife "epitomizes a family value," usually tries to work her into his speeches.
4/13/89

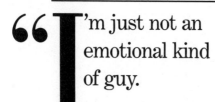

I'm just not an emotional kind of guy.

— 9/9/89

If I show some emotion, that's just the way I am.

— 6/6/91

I'm not too good at the emotional side.

— 10/27/90

We Bushes cry easily.

— 9/5/89

If occasionally I do go up in smoke, it doesn't relate to this line of work.

— 12/3/89

MR. SENSITIVITY

'**O**bviously, when you see somebody go berserk and get a weapon and go in and murder people, of course, it troubles me.'

—on the Killeen massacre, in which a lone gunman murdered 23 people in a Texas cafeteria. Though troubled, Bush did not see the tragedy as reason to rethink his opposition to gun control.
10/17/91

66 **H**igh tech is potent, precise, and in the end, unbeatable. The truth is, it reminds a lot of people of the way I pitch horseshoes. Would you believe some of the people? Would you believe our dog? Look, I want to give the high-five symbol to high tech. 99

—at the Ford Aerospace Space Systems Division, Palo Alto, California, on the importance of high-tech and his support for a capital gains tax break. 4/25/89

‘I've got to run now and relax. The doctor told me to relax. The doctor told me to relax. The doctor told me. He was the one. He said, 'Relax.' ”

—upon arrival at Andrews Air Force Base, ending a press conference. Bush heeded his physician's advice on this occasion, but ignored it during a later trip to Japan, with unfortunate results for Japanese Prime Minister Miyazawa's suit.
5/12/91

STRAWBERRY FIELDS

---

66 **S**omebody—somebody asked me, what's it take to win? I said to them, I can't remember, what does it take to win the Super Bowl? Or maybe Steinbrenner, my friend George, will tell us what it takes for the Yanks to win—one run. But I went over to the Strawberry Festival this morning, and ate a piece of shortcake over there—able to enjoy it right away, and once I completed it, it didn't have to be approved by Congress—I just went ahead and ate it—and that leads me into what I want to talk to you about today.... 99

—at a Bush-Quayle fund-raising luncheon in Tampa, Florida. Bush, who had already made the shortcake joke earlier in the day with markedly greater success, went on to talk about family values.
3/4/92

' **G**et this [economic plan] passed. Later on, we can all debate it. **99**

— during his remarks to the New Hampshire State Legislature in Concord, Bush appeals to Congress to pass his economic growth package.
2/12/92

" I mean a child that doesn't have a parent to read to that child or that doesn't see that when the child is hurting to have a parent and help out or neither parent there enough to pick the kid up and dust him off and send him back into the game at school or whatever, that kid has a disadvantage. "

—in an interview with David Frost, on the importance of the family. 1/3/92

‘ I put confidence in the
American people, in
their ability to sort
through what is fair and
what is unfair, what is ugly
and what is unugly. ’’

> —at a White House press
> conference, defending himself
> against charges of negative
> campaigning during the '88
> elections. (Bush then offered
> his ultimate defense of his
> campaign advertisements: "I
> was elected.")
> 11/7/89

> **I**'ve had no indication from home, nor have we picked up any here that they felt that the U.S. economy was going to move towards a recession.

—7/16/89

> The economy is moving in the right direction.

—10/4/91

> I don't want to buy into the predicate about [the U.S. being in] another recession. I don't feel that way.

—10/25/91

> The economy's turned the corner, headed for recovery.

—10/31/91

I'm not prepared to say we are in a recession.

— 11/8/91

It will not be a deep recession.

— 1/4/92

This economy is in free-fall.

— 1/15/92

"**W**hen I need a little free advice about Saddam Hussein, I turn to country music. "

—at a country music awards ceremony in Nashville, Tennessee. Bush also turns to country music when he's on the campaign trail. In New Hampshire, he quoted lyrics from a song by the Nitty Gritty Dirt Band, but had some trouble with the group's name, referring to them as the "Nitty Ditty Nitty Gritty Great Bird." 10/2/91

FOR WHOM THE BELL KNELLS

"I don't want to get, you know, here we are close to the election—sounding a knell of overconfidence that I don't feel. "

> — in a David Frost interview with candidate Bush, seeking to avoid making predictions based on his winning the election. 11/6/88

---

66 I happen to be one who has learned in one short year that faith is important, and I think we got—I have a philosophy of what happened, a theory. We came out of the Vietnam War. It was very divisive. We had that post-Watergate period that increased a certain national cynicism, it seemed to me, and that spills off on young people, maybe on their teachers. So, we're now coming into a new period. We look around the world, and we see the darndest, most dramatic changes moving towards the values that—that have made this country the greatest, freedom, democracy, choice to do things—you know. 99

— meeting with students at Taft
High School in Cincinnati, Ohio,
on the changes that are moving
American teens away from
alienation and hopelessness.
1/12/90

THOSE NAZI GUYS

'Boy, they were big on crematoriums, weren't they?'

— during a tour of Auschwitz.
9/28/87

27

66 The concept of the Dukakis family has my great respect. 99

— during the Bush-Dukakis presidential debate in Los Angeles, when asked if he had anything nice to say about his opponent.
10/13/88

'**W**e've been in touch. And some of the—some of the things are very good. Ah—I'm trying to think— There were several things, maybe one of them was the <u>Iowa</u>, when those kids lost their lives, maybe, I think it was. If it wasn't, it was something else dealing with the lives of young Americans in a very sensitive and thoughtful letter; and he, I got word from him at the time of the earthquake, very warm and sentimental and convincingly real response and gratitude, just for that little show of interest, you see. ''

— during an interview with David Frost, on his correspondence from and to Gorbachev. Although the two kept in touch, Bush was far from prescient on Gorbachev's fate, asserting in June 1991: "We, for the United States, do not anticipate his demise in any way." 9/5/89

"We have—I have—want to be positioned in that I could not possibly support David Duke, because of the racism and because of the ... bigotry and all of this."

— during a White House press conference, distancing himself from the Republican candidate for governor of Louisiana. Bush later dismissed Duke as an "insincere charlatan." 10/25/91

MAJOR MAJOR

'**I** think there were some differences, there's no question, and will still be. We're talking about a major, major situation here ... I mean, we've got a major rapport—relationship of economics, major in the security, and all of that, we should not lose sight of. **"**

— during a press conference aboard Air Force One before takeoff from Japan, on his trade talks with Prime Minister Miyazawa and the need for perseverance.
1/10/92

---

66 **I**t's no exaggeration to
say the undecideds could
go one way or another. 99

— at a campaign rally in Troy,
Ohio, speculating to local
voters that Ohio's twenty-three
electoral college votes might
be the "swing votes" that would
determine the entire election.
10/21/88

6 6 To kind of suddenly try to get my hair colored, and dance up and down in a miniskirt or do something, you know, show that I've got a lot of jazz out there and drop a bunch of one-liners, I'm running for the president of the United States . . . I kind of think I'm a scintillating kind of fellow. 9 9

— defending his own particular brand of charisma to reporters in Ohio during a campaign stop. Bush asserted that the voters weren't looking for "pizazz." "What's wrong with being a boring kind of guy?" he asked. 4/26/88

66 **W**e have a complicated
three-way
conundrum at this
point. 99

—during a press briefing in
Houston, Texas, on the difficulty
of restoring the economy of
postinvasion Panama while
ensuring democracy and
respecting the country's
sovereignty.
12/30/89

BUSH: Let me be clear, I'm not in favor of new taxes. I'll repeat that over and over and over again. And this one compromise that—where we begrudgingly had to accept revenues, revenue increases, is the exception that proves the rule....

REPORTER: The exception that proves what rule?

BUSH: The rule that I'm strongly opposed to raising taxes.

—at a press conference in Honolulu, Hawaii, defending his decision to break his "no new taxes" pledge. Later, he justified his change of heart to reporters: "I'm doing like Lincoln did, 'Think anew.' I'm thinking anew." 10/27/90

---

66 **S**he refurbished the White House with the dignity that is her legacy. 99

—on former First Lady Nancy Reagan, at the dedication of the Reagan Library in Simi, California.
11/4/91

‘‘My running mate took the lead, was the author, of the Job Training Partnership Act. Now, because of a lot of smoke and frenzying of bluefish out there, going after a drop of blood in the water, nobody knows that.’’

— on NBC-TV's *Today* show, defending his vice presidential nominee. Bush also defended his choice of Quayle with, "There's something very exciting about putting some confidence in someone in his 30s or 40s."
11/3/88

66 **A**nd let me say in conclusion, thanks for the kids. I learned an awful lot about bathtub toys—about how to work the telephone. One guy knows—several of them know their own phone numbers—preparation to go to the dentist. A lot of things I'd forgotten. So it' been a good day. 99

—at the Emily Harns Head Start
Center in Catonsville, Marylan
1/21/92

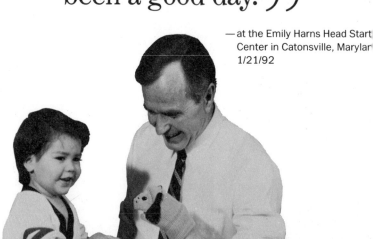

"This is not a tax break for the rich, it is a creation of small jobs."

— during a roundtable discussion with New Hampshire community leaders while campaigning at Pease Air Force Base, NH, on his time-worn proposal to stimulate growth by cutting the capital gains tax.
1/15/92

66 All I was doing was appealing for an endorsement, not suggesting you endorse it. 99

— to Roy Romer, governor of Colorado, at a meeting of the National Governors Association. After Bush detailed his economic growth proposal to the governors, Romer had attacked the plan as partisan and not reflecting the position of many governors. 2/3/92

AND THE FIRST AMENDMENT HELPED TOO

---

66 I was shot down, and I was floating around in a little yellow raft, setting a record for paddling. I thought of my family, my mom and dad, and the strength I got from them. I thought of my faith, the separation of church and state. 99

— in a speech at the Old Creamery Theatre in Garrison, Ohio, relating his experiences as a World War II fighter pilot. 12/5/87

" **A**nd I guess with these cameras listening, be sure never to end your sentence with a—without—end a sentence with a preposition because it will be duly reported all across the country by these guardians of the —. "

—meeting with Close-Up Foundation Students at the White House, offering the students a quick grammar lesson.
3/29/89

'Fluency in English is something that I'm often not accused of. 99

— toasting Pakistani Prime Minister Benazir Bhutto at a White House dinner. Despite his lack of fluency, however, the president insists on controlling the content of his speeches, "inarticulate as though I may be."
6/6/89

"Almost every place you can point, contrary to Mr. Mondale's—I gotta be careful—but contrary of how he goes around just saying everything bad. If somebody sees a silver lining, he finds a big black cloud out there. Whine on harvest moon! I mean, there's a lot going on, a lot of opportunity."

— during the vice presidential debate, defending Reagan's social services record from Mondale's "carping" negativism. 10/11/84

'Please just don't look at part of the glass, the part that is only less than half full. 99

— during a news conference before his departure for Rome to attend a NATO summit, on the bright side of the previous day's gubernatorial elections, which saw his friend Dick Thornburgh defeated in Pennsylvania.
11/6/91

BARBARA: I think it's because I don't threaten anybody. I don't make any big decisions, I'm trying to say this nicely so I won't hurt my own feelings. But—I mean—no Marilyn Monroe am I. I'm just not a threat to anybody. I like people. And I feel for them. Maybe more than I should that's good for me.

GEORGE: Maybe Joe DiMaggio disagrees with you.

BARBARA: What's that mean? Marilyn Monroe?

GEORGE: I think—Marilyn Monroe—maybe has the same high regard.

BARBARA: Well, that's nice.

—during an interview with David Frost. Barbara was attempting to explain why so many people seem to relate to her. 9/5/89

"**N**o, you're not going to see me stay put ... I am not going to forsake my responsibilities. You may not see me put as much—I mean, un-put as much. "

—at a news conference after the NATO summit in Rome, clarifying travel plans for the coming year. Bush had just announced the cancellation of a planned trip to Japan. 11/8/91

EYE CONTACT

66 I had an opportunity to thank him eyeball-to-eyeball for the best communications I believe any two countries could possibly have had. 99

—at a press conference following his meeting at Camp David with President Turgut Ozal of Turkey, on the two countries' cooperation during the Gulf war.
3/23/91

‘Y ou need to be able to do more than 'just say no.' You need to have the confidence to look your false friends in the eyes and say, 'Hell, no, I don't want any of that.' ,,

—at an antidrug rally in Denver, Colorado, expounding on the "refusal skills" required for modern teens to combat peer pressure. Bush may have been hoping to save these youngsters from, as he once put it, the "narced-up terrorist kind of guys." 12/8/89

"**U**p and down. It started with trauma—
to go or not to go, in terms of the use
of military force in Kuwait, the Persian
Gulf area, in order to kick Saddam
Hussein out. And so that started with tension.
And shortly thereafter, fantastic conclusion to
that war. And then a long, kind of slow,
sluggish economy that hurt a lot of people and
ended—oh, and of course, inside of that, the
change, the coup in the Soviet Union this
summer. . . . So it was a year of mixed

emotions, and ending with good news today on the economic front, but still, with a very sluggish economy, good news in the sense that the Fed has lowered the rates to almost historic lows, which should have a stimulative effect on the economy. So it's been a year of up and down. On a personal side, of course, great happiness for me and Barbara, sadness in that our house got clobbered, but when I look at that and think of some of the hardship of the American people and I can say we've been very lucky. **99**

— summing up the past year
during a C-SPAN interview
12/22/91

66 **W**e're delighted to be here, Barbara and I. There's a danger: You have President Reagan, Governor Deukmejian, and George Bush. Watch out— Overdose of charisma! That's not too good. 99

—at a campaign rally in Los Angeles, California. "I think I'm a charismatic son of a gun," the Republican presidential nominee admitted on another occasion, but, he went on, "I'm not going to depend entirely on that to win."
8/24/88

A LITTLE BIT PRO-LIFE

'' **W**ell, it appear to a double standard to some, but I—that's my position, and it's—we don't have the time to philosophically discuss it here, but ... we're going to opt on the side of life. And that is—that is the—that really is the underlying part of this for me. You know, I mentioned—and with really from the heart—this concept of going across the river to this little church and watching one of our children—adopted kid—be baptized. And that made for me—it was very emotional for me. It helped me in reaching a very personal view of this question. And I don't know. ''

—at a press conference with president-elect Bush to announce new Cabinet appointments. Bush was responding to a criticism that his position supporting prosecution of abortionists but not of women choosing abortion represented a double standard. 12/22/88

TAKE YOUR TIME, DON'T RUSH

" **I** know what I've told you I'm going to say, I'm going to say. And what else I say, well, I'll take some time to figure out— figure that all out. "

—at a joint news conference with President Louis Alberto Lacalle of Uruguay, on the message he was planning to deliver to Iraqi Foreign Minister Tariq Aziz. Later, asked if there were room for a face-saving measure, Bush was adamant: "I don't care about face! He doesn't need any face!" 12/4/90

"And the other thing, and I guess—is that I expect it's difficult for somebody working in a plant here in New Hampshire to wonder, to know if the president really cares about what's happening in the economy. And I think I know this state. I went to school a thousand years ago across the border and—would go up every summer of my life, except 1944, to Maine, spending a fair amount of time. Almost—you could see it, practically, coming in on the plane. So when you get clobbered on the seacoast by a storm, I get clobbered on the seacoast by a storm. It goes further than that. When you get hurting because you worry whether you're going to have a job or you get thrown out, I do care about it and I just wanted to say that."

— to disgruntled employees of Davidson Textron during a campaign stop in Dover, New Hampshire.
1/15/92

55

Watch quite a bit. I watch the news and I don't like to tell you this, because you'll think I'm into some weird TV freak here, but we—I have a set upstairs that has five screens on it and I can sit on my desk and whip—just punch a button if I see one off on the corner, that moves into the middle screen, the other one goes to the side. Then I can run up and down the—up and down the dial. So I—and you can record all four—four going at once, while you—when you're watching. I don't quite know how to do that yet. But I cite this because Barbara accuses me of being too much—not too much, but plugged into TV too often, put it that way. Love sports on TV.

— during a C-SPAN interview with the president, on his preferred pastimes.
12/22/91

'Hey, hey, nihaoma. Hey, yeah, yeah. Heil, heil—a kind of Hitler salute.'

— greeting international tourists at Lafayette Park on his way home from church. (Nihaoma is Mandarin for "how are you?") 3/29/92

66 **T**hose are two hypo-rhetorical questions. 99

— during the Bush-Dukakis presidential debate, probing Dukakis' defense policy. 9/25/88

66 **I**'m not going to hypothecate that it may—anything goes too fast. 99

— at a question-and-answer session in the Oval Office, on the speed of reforms in Eastern Europe. 9/9/89

'These, they're very dangerous. They trap you. Especially these furry ones...it's these furry guys that get you in real trouble. They can reach out and listen to something so—keep it respectful here. '

—at a photo opportunity with his fitness czar, Arnold Schwarzenegger, on the need for caution when speaking near open microphones. 9/13/91

66 I'm for Mr. Reagan— blindly. 99

—while campaigning in
Manhattan.
11/1/84

66 I will never apologize for the United States of America, ever. I don't care what the facts are. 99

—to the Bush '88 Coalition of
American Nationalities in
Washington, confirming his
contention that "I'm not an
apologize-for-America kind of
guy."
8/2/88

'I don't know whether I'd call it 'cashing in.' I expect every president has written his memoirs and received money for it. Indeed, I read that a former president—was it Grant? Grant got half a million bucks—that's when half a million really meant something.'

— at a White House press conference, defending Reagan against charges that the reputed $5 million Reagan had negotiated for his autobiography represented cashing in on the presidency.
1/27/89

---

66 The Democrats choked the throttle—pulled the throttle back of a slowing economy while they hunted for every last morsel of partisan advantage. 99

— at a fund-raiser for Bill Price held at the Cowboy Hall of Fame in Oklahoma City, Oklahoma, taking the Democrats to task for delaying a budget agreement. 10/29/90

GOBBLE, GOBBLE

'Let me see whether I dare read you this. 'Dear George:'—this is from President Reagan—'You'll have moments when you want to use this particular stationery. Well, go to it. George, I treasure the memories we share, and wish you all the very best. You'll be in my prayers. God bless you and Barbara. I'll miss our Thursday lunches. Ron.' And the heading on the paper is, 'Don't let the turkeys get you down.' So, nobody here should take personal this at all. I mean this is a broad, ecumenical statement. 'Do not let the turkeys get you down.' And it shows a bunch of turkeys trying to get an elephant down. Then it says 'Boynton' on the bottom.'

—during his first presidential press conference.
1/21/89

> **"I** mean, I think there'll be a lot of aftermaths in what happened, but we're going to go forward. **"**

—at a press conference announcing Dick Cheney as the new nominee for secretary of defense after John Tower's rejection in the Senate. Only three weeks before, Bush had told reporters, "I know of nobody else [besides Tower] whose knowledge . . . can equal his. So he is my choice, my only choice." If Cheney felt cheapened, he didn't say. 3/10/89

IF THEY KILL TWO, IT'S TERRIBLE

'Look, if an American Marine is killed—if they kill an American Marine, that's real bad. And if they threaten and brutalize the wife of an American citizen, sexually threatening the lieutenant's wife while kicking him in the groin over and over again, then, Mr. Gorbachev, please understand, this president is going to do something about it. "

—at a White House press conference, asked how he would justify his invasion of Panama to the Soviet leader. 12/21/89

66 I don't know that it would be my judgment—my—the function of the president to suggest what employment somebody should take. If you ask me, would I like to go out there, leave my job and go to work for this sheik when I get through being president, no, I wouldn't like to do that. 99

—at a press conference on Sununu aide Edward Rogers' possible conflict of interest in accepting a position with a Saudi sheik for a reputed $600,000 compensation despite having absolutely no experience in the private sector. 10/25/91

> **❝I** saw a story yesterday that I went a little ballistic—which is only part true—semi-ballistic. **❞**

—at a press conference announcing John Tower as the nominee for secretary of defense, on news stories impugning Tower's character. Bush went on to predict, "This matter is now totally concluded." Three months later, Tower was rejected by the full Senate.
12/16/88

66 I've got to be careful I don't overcheerlead on this economy. 99

—during an interview with a local
station in Houston, Texas,
expressing caution lest his
optimism about the state of the
economy be mistaken for
indifference to the plight of the
unemployed.
11/1/91

SOMEONE MOVED THE GOAL POSTS

"Well, I'm going to kick that one right into the end zone of the secretary of education. But, yes, we have all—he travels a good deal, goes abroad. We have a lot of people in the department that does that. We're having an international—this is not as much education as dealing with the environment—a big international conference coming up. And we get it all the time—exchanges of ideas. But I think we've got—we set out there—and I want to give credit to your Governor McWherter and to your former governor Lamar Alexander—we've gotten great ideas for a national goals program from—in this country— from the governors who were responding to, maybe, the principal of your high school, for heaven's sake."

—at the University of Tennessee, Knoxville, with Education Secretary Lauro Cavazos. Bush was responding to a student's question about turning to other countries for ideas on education reform.
2/2/90

ROLE MODELS

"I don't really think I—I think I respected certain components of one's presidency—Lincoln for his fairness, his determination, I'm going to preserve the Union. Then his equity that came with the freeing of the slaves. That's so big and so strong that obviously it had to be inspiring. Teddy Roosevelt's commitment to the great outdoors, and his, you know, kind of zest for life. His kids were around this very lawn out here. We have ours out there now. I mean, there's some examples of that kind. In fact, I'm not going to be driven off the golf course. Didn't affect Ike, and it isn't going to affect me either. I can do two things at once—mind the country's business and then every once in a while play golf. So I— I think there's a lot of examples in previous presidencies, pros and cons. **"**

— during a C-SPAN interview with the president. Bush was asked about the influence of previous presidents on his own tenure in office.
12/22/91

"Look, how was the actual deployment thing?"

— to astronauts aboard the space shuttle *Atlantis*. Bush then invited the astronauts to the White House to "see the new puppies."
5/9/89

---

66 **I**'ve been talking the same way for years, so it can't be that serious. 99

—at a news conference after attending church in Kennebunkport, Maine. Could Bush improve his oratorical skills with practice? "Can't act," explained the President. "Just have to be me."
8/7/88

‘‘ I just am not one who—
who flamboyantly
believes in throwing a lot
of words around. ’’

—at a press conference in Kennebunkport, Maine, on his reluctance to call U.S. interference with Iraqi shipping a "blockade." Bush was concerned that this might give the wrong impression. 8/11/90

❝ I'm all for Lawrence Welk. Lawrence Welk is a wonderful man. He used to be, or was, or—wherever he is now, bless him. ❞

—at an "Ask George Bush" question-and-answer session during a campaign stop at Brookline High School, Hollis, NH. Bush, arguing for presidential line-item veto power to stop pork barrel spending projects such as the proposed Lawrence Welk Museum, apparently didn't know whether Welk was alive or dead.
2/16/92

GIVE THAT GUY AN NEA GRANT

'Ours is a great state, and we don't like limits of any kind. Ricky Clunn is one of the great bass fishermen. He's a Texas young guy, and he's a very competitive fisherman, and he talked about learning to fish wading in the creeks behind his dad. He in his underwear went wading in the creeks behind his father, and he said—as a fisherman he said it's great to grow up in a country with no limits.'

—at a livestock and rodeo event in Houston, Texas. Bush, born and raised in the East, can get defensive about his credentials as a Texan: "I have my Texas hunting license here...." 2/28/92

> " **A**nd I would say to those out around the country, 'Take a hard look now. Don't let that rabbit be pulled out of the hat by one hand and 25 other rabbits dumped on you in another.' "

— at a White House press conference, illustrating his contention that a tax proposal by Senator Moynihan of New York to eliminate the Social Security surplus amounts to a "sleight of hand operation, here."
1/24/90

'We've got the best health care plan there is and it does not socialize medicine in this country. It preserves the quality of care. It makes health care—gives health care access to all and it does it without reducing the quality of American education.'

—during an early-morning stroll among the cherry blossoms. 4/8/92

"I say the same thing I say to a person whose family was maimed by a pistol or an explosive charge or whatever else it might be—a fire—this is bad. **"**

— during a White House press conference, on his response to families of victims of gun violence. Bush went on to lament the difficulties of trying to put limits on AK-47 assault rifles "and still, you know, do what's right by the legitimate sportsman."
3/7/89

❝There's no difference between me and the president on taxes. No more nitpicking. Zip-ah-dee-doo-dah. Now, it's off to the races!❞

— in Denver, responding to criticism that differences between himself and Reagan on tax issues were creating a political liability for the incumbents.
8/8/84

> **So far it did not reverberate in the negative there. The signature is being checked through the master computer, which is located someplace else, and we'll get an answer back after we leave.**

—using a signature-verifier at a National Grocers Association convention in Orlando, Florida. This was the same convention at which Bush made his legendary gaffe upon viewing a supermarket price scanner: "This is for checking out?" 2/4/92

BUSH: It's a jungle out there.

REPORTER: Are you getting frustrated with Gorbachev?

BUSH: Did you hear about Tarzan and Jane?

REPORTER: No.

BUSH: Tarzan came down and he said, "Jane, I'll have a double. On the rocks." She said, "Tarzan, you don't..." "I'll have another double on the rocks." He has a third drink. Jane says, "What's the matter, Tarzan." He says, "It's a jungle out there." Get it?

REPORTER: Yeah.

> —at an informal golf-course news conference in Kennebunkport, expressing his frustration with incessant questioning by the press. Bush likes to be left alone when he is on vacation at his "ancestral home," as he once put it.
> 7/6/91

66 So it's trying to find this common ground and catch this wave, this wave that's moving through Eastern Europe, and indeed around the world, of freedom and democracy and things of that nature. 99

—during a pre-European trip press conference, on facilitating changes in the Eastern bloc. 6/6/89

GLUG, GLUG, GLUG

'' So tomorrow there'll be another tidal wave, so keep your snorkel above the water level and do what you think is right. ''

— during a question-and-answer session aboard *Air Force One*, on forthcoming budget negotiations.
5/11/90

' You know, every day, many important papers come across the desk in that marvelous Oval Office, and very few items remain there for long. Got to keep that paper moving or you get inundated. Your snorkel will fill up and there will be no justice. ''

— in remarks before the Disabled American Veterans in Washington, D.C., on the difficulty of keeping up with his presidential duties.
9/12/91

66 It's like Missouri, 'Show me.' I'm from Missouri; we've got to see exactly what's going on. 99

—at a White House press conference, on Iraq's claims to be complying with U.N. resolutions demanding destruction of military equipment in the wake of the Gulf war.
7/10/91

'I think in politics there are certain moral values. I'm one who—we believe strongly in separation of church and state, but when you get into some questions, there are some moral overtones. Murder, that kind of thing, and I feel a little, I will say, uncomfortable with the elevation of the religion thing.'

— on the TV show *Meet the Press*, on the tension between religion and politics. In the 1984 vice presidential debate, Bush explained his position on church-state issues this way: "We don't believe in denominationally moving in." 9/16/84

66 **W**e've got a little toy department to look at to get some stuff for the grandchildren. 'Slime' is the name of it, I believe. It's a toy. 99

—at the Frederick Towne Mall in Frederick, MD, doing some Christmas shopping. Bush then went off in search of "that Slime thing." 11/29/91

'' Thank you all very much. And let me just say this, on a personal basis. I've screwed up a couple of times here and I'm very grateful for your assistance in straightening it out. God, I'd hate to have had some of those answers stand. ''

—at a press conference
8/8/90

CREDITS

Front cover photo UPI/Bettmann
Back cover photo AP/Wide World Photos

Photographs on pages 1, 11, 20, 24, 40, 75, 83 UPI/Bettmann

Photographs on pages 2, 5, 7, 8, 12, 15, 17, 23, 29, 33, 34, 38, 45, 47, 48, 50, 53, 54, 59, 63, 64, 68, 71, 79, 84, 87 AP/Wide World Photos

The quotations in this book were compiled from the following sources: the Federal News Service, the Associated Press, the Washington *Post*, *The Wall Street Journal*, C-SPAN, the Washington *Times*, *Time*, *Newsweek*, and official White House Press Office transcripts

YOU LOVE THE BOOK.
WAIT 'TIL YOU SEE THE
MAGAZINE!

"Bushisms" are only a fraction of what *The New Republic* does best. Subscribe now and get a weekly dose of the wit and wisdom of Mike Kinsley, Fred Barnes, Andrew Sullivan, Morton Kondracke, Michael Lewis, Jacob Weisberg, and a host of other entertaining writers. Winner of the National Magazine Award for General Excellence, *The New Republic* is America's best journal of opinion.

To subscribe just fill in this card, detach and mail it before December 31, 1992. Or for fastest service call 1-800-274-6350. Offer expires December 31, 1992.

☐ **Yes!** Send me 48 issues of *The New Republic* for only $34.99 (50% off the basic rate).

Name _____

Address _____ Apt. _____

City _____ State _____ Zip _____

☐ Payment Enclosed
☐ Bill Me Later
For new subscribers only. Allow 3-5 weeks for delivery. Offer for U.S. addresses only.

Please charge my ☐ Visa ☐ MC ☐ AMEX
Account # _____

Expiration date _____ Interbank _____

Signature _____

5BOK1

THE NEW REPUBLIC

New Order
Process Immediately

BUSINESS REPLY MAIL
FIRST CLASS MAIL   PERMIT NO. 1276   BOULDER, CO

POSTAGE WILL BE PAID BY ADDRESSEE

THE
NEW REPUBLIC
Subscription Department
Post Office Box 56515
Boulder, CO 80321-6515